CONVENTION BETWEEN
THE GOVERNMENT OF THE UNITED STATES OF AMERICA AND
THE GOVERNMENT OF JAPAN
FOR THE AVOIDANCE OF DOUBLE TAXATION
AND THE PREVENTION OF FISCAL EVASION
WITH RESPECT TO TAXES ON INCOME

The Government of the United States of America and the Government of Japan,

Desiring to conclude a new Convention for the avoidance of double taxation and the prevention of fiscal evasion with respect to taxes on income,

Have agreed as follows:

ARTICLE 1

1.   This Convention shall apply only to persons who are residents of one or both of the Contracting States, except as otherwise provided in the Convention.

2.   The provisions of this Convention shall not be construed to restrict in any manner any exclusion, exemption, deduction, credit, or other allowance now or hereafter accorded:

(a)   by the laws of a Contracting State in the determination of the tax imposed by that Contracting State; or

(b)   by any other bilateral agreement between the Contracting States or any multilateral agreement to which the Contracting States are parties.

3.   (a)   Notwithstanding the provisions of subparagraph (b) of paragraph 2:

(i)   any question arising as to the interpretation or application of this Convention and, in particular, whether a measure is within the scope of this Convention, shall be determined exclusively in accordance with the provisions of Article 25 of this Convention; and

(ii)   the provisions of Article XVII of the General Agreement on Trade in Services shall not apply to a measure unless the competent authorities agree that the measure is not within the scope of Article 24 of this Convention.

(b)   For the purposes of this paragraph, the term "measure" means a law, regulation, rule, procedure, decision, administrative action, or any similar provision or action, as related to taxes of every kind and description imposed by a Contracting State without regard to Article 2 and subparagraph (d) of paragraph 1 of Article 3.

4.   (a)   Except to the extent provided in paragraph 5, this Convention shall not affect the taxation by a Contracting State of its residents (as determined under Article 4) and, in the case of the United States, its citizens.

(b)   Notwithstanding the other provisions of this Convention, a former citizen or long-term resident of the United States may, for the period of ten years following the loss of such status, be taxed in accordance with the laws of the United States, if the loss of such status had as one of its principal purposes the avoidance of tax (as defined under the laws of the United States).

5.   The provisions of paragraph 4 shall not affect the benefits conferred by a Contracting State under paragraphs 2 and 3 of Article 9, paragraph 3 of Article 17, and Articles 18, 19, 20, 23, 24, 25 and 28, but in the case of benefits conferred by the United States under Articles 18, 19 and 20 only if the individuals claiming the benefits are neither citizens of, nor have been lawfully admitted for permanent residence in, the United States.

ARTICLE 2

1.   This Convention shall apply to the following taxes:

(a)   in the case of Japan:

(i)   the income tax; and

(ii)   the corporation tax

(hereinafter referred to as "Japanese tax");

(b)   in the case of the United States, the Federal income taxes imposed by the Internal Revenue Code but excluding social security taxes (hereinafter referred to as "United States tax").

2.   This Convention shall also apply to any identical or substantially similar taxes which are imposed after the date of signature of the Convention in addition to, or in place of, those referred to in paragraph 1. The competent authorities of the Contracting States shall notify each other of any substantial changes which have been made in their respective tax laws, or changes in other laws that significantly affect their obligations under the Convention, within a reasonable period of time after such changes.

ARTICLE 3

1.   For the purposes of this Convention, unless the context otherwise requires:

(a)   the term "Japan", when used in a geographical sense, means all the territory of Japan, including its territorial sea, in which the laws relating to Japanese tax are in force, and all the area beyond its territorial sea, including the seabed and subsoil thereof, over which Japan has jurisdiction in accordance with international law and in which the laws relating to Japanese tax are in force;

(b)   the term "United States" means the United States of America. When used in a geographical sense, the term includes the states thereof and the District of Columbia; such term also includes the territorial sea thereof and the seabed and subsoil of the submarine areas adjacent to that territorial sea, over which the United States exercises sovereign rights in accordance with international law; the term, however, does not include Puerto Rico, the Virgin Islands, Guam or any other United States possession or territory;

(c)   the terms "a Contracting State" and "the other Contracting State" mean Japan or the United States, as the context requires;

(d)   the term "tax" means Japanese tax or United States tax, as the context requires;

(e)   the term "person" includes an individual, a company and any other body of persons;

(f)   the term "company" means any body corporate or any entity that is treated as a body corporate for tax purposes;

(g)   the term "enterprise" applies to the carrying on of any business;

(h)   the terms "enterprise of a Contracting State" and "enterprise of the other Contracting State" mean respectively an enterprise carried on by a resident of a Contracting State and an enterprise carried on by a resident of the other Contracting State;

(i)   the term "international traffic" means any transport by a ship or aircraft operated by an enterprise of a Contracting State, except when such transport is solely between places in the other Contracting State;

(j)   the term "national" of a Contracting State means:

    (i)   in relation to Japan, any individual possessing the nationality of Japan and any juridical person or other organization deriving its status as such from the laws in force in Japan; and

(ii)   in relation to the United States, any individual possessing the citizenship of the United States and any legal person, partnership or association deriving its status as such from the laws in force in the United States;

(k)   the term "competent authority" means:

(i)   in the case of Japan, the Minister of Finance or his authorized representative; and

(ii)   in the case of the United States, the Secretary of the Treasury or his delegate;

(l)   the term "business" includes the performance of professional services and of other activities of an independent character; and

(m)   the term "pension fund" means any person that:

(i)   is organized under the laws of a Contracting State;

(ii)   is established and maintained in that Contracting State primarily to administer or provide pensions or other similar remuneration, including social security payments; and

(iii)   is exempt from tax in that Contracting State with respect to the activities described in clause (ii).

2.   As regards the application of this Convention at any time by a Contracting State any term not defined therein shall, unless the context otherwise requires, or the competent authorities agree otherwise on the meaning of a term for the purposes of applying the Convention pursuant to Article 25, have the meaning which it has at that time under the laws of that Contracting State for the purposes of the taxes to which the Convention applies, any meaning under the applicable tax laws of that Contracting State prevailing over a meaning given to the term under other laws of that Contracting State.

ARTICLE 4

1.   For the purposes of this Convention, the term "resident of a Contracting State" means any person who, under the laws of that Contracting State, is liable to tax therein by reason of

his domicile, residence, citizenship, place of head or main office, place of incorporation, or any other criterion of a similar nature, and also includes:

(a)   that Contracting State and any political subdivision or local authority thereof;

(b)   a pension fund organized under the laws of that Contracting State; and

(c)   a person organized under the laws of that Contracting State and established and maintained in that Contracting State exclusively for a religious, charitable, educational, scientific, artistic, cultural or public purpose, even if the person is exempt from tax in that Contracting State.

This term, however, does not include any person who is liable to tax in that Contracting State in respect only of income from sources in that Contracting State, or of profits attributable to a permanent establishment in that Contracting State.

2.   Notwithstanding the provisions of paragraph 1, an individual who is a United States citizen or an alien lawfully admitted for permanent residence in the United States under the laws of the United States shall be regarded as a resident of the United States only if the individual:

(a)   is not a resident of Japan under paragraph 1;

(b)   has a substantial presence, permanent home or habitual abode in the United States; and

(c)   for the purposes of a convention or agreement for the avoidance of double taxation between Japan and a state other than the United States, is not a resident of that state.

3.   Where by reason of the provisions of paragraph 1 an individual not described in paragraph 2 is a resident of both Contracting States, then his status shall be determined as follows:

(a)   he shall be deemed to be a resident of the Contracting State in which he has a permanent home available to him; if he has a permanent home available to him in both Contracting States, he shall be deemed to be a resident of the Contracting State with which his personal and economic relations are closer (center of vital interests);

(b)   if the Contracting State in which he has his center of vital interests cannot be determined, or if he does not have a permanent home available to him in either Contracting State, he shall be deemed to be a resident of the Contracting State in which he has an habitual abode;

(c)   if he has an habitual abode in both Contracting States or in neither of them, he shall be deemed to be a resident of the Contracting State of which he is a national;

(d)   if he is a national of both Contracting States or of neither of them, the competent authorities of the Contracting States shall settle the question by mutual agreement.

An individual who is deemed to be a resident of a Contracting State by reason of the provisions of this paragraph shall be deemed to be a resident only of that Contracting State for the purposes of this Convention.

4.   Where by reason of the provisions of paragraph 1 a person other than an individual is a resident of both Contracting States, then the competent authorities of the Contracting States shall determine by mutual agreement the Contracting State of which that person shall be deemed to be a resident for the purposes of this Convention. In the absence of a mutual agreement by the competent authorities of the Contracting States, the person shall not be considered a resident of either Contracting State for the purposes of claiming any benefits provided by the Convention.

5.   Where, pursuant to any provision of this Convention, a Contracting State reduces the rate of tax on, or exempts from tax, income of a resident of the other Contracting State and under the laws in force in that other Contracting State the resident is subject to tax by that other Contracting State only on that part of such income which is remitted to or received in that other Contracting State, then the reduction or exemption shall apply only to so much of such income as is remitted to or received in that other Contracting State.

6.   For the purposes of applying this Convention:

(a)   An item of income:

(i)   derived from a Contracting State through an entity that is organized in the other Contracting State; and

(ii)   treated as the income of the beneficiaries, members or participants of that entity under the tax laws of that other Contracting State;

shall be eligible for the benefits of the Convention that would be granted if it were directly derived by a beneficiary, member or participant of that entity who is a resident of that other Contracting State, to the extent that such beneficiaries, members or participants are residents of that other Contracting State and satisfy any other conditions specified in the Convention, without regard to whether the income is treated as the income of such beneficiaries, members or participants under the tax laws of the first-mentioned Contracting State.

(b)   An item of income:

(i)   derived from a Contracting State through an entity that is organized in the other Contracting State; and

(ii)   treated as the income of that entity under the tax laws of that other Contracting State;

shall be eligible for the benefits of the Convention that would be granted to a resident of that other Contracting State, without regard to whether the income is treated as the income of the entity under the tax laws of the first-mentioned Contracting State, if such entity is a resident of that other Contracting State and satisfies any other conditions specified in the Convention.

(c)   An item of income:

(i)   derived from a Contracting State through an entity that is organized in a state other than the Contracting States; and

(ii)   treated as the income of the beneficiaries, members or participants of that entity under the tax laws of the other Contracting State;

shall be eligible for the benefits of the Convention that would be granted if it were directly derived by a beneficiary, member or participant of that entity who is a resident of that other Contracting State, to the extent that such beneficiaries, members or participants are residents of that other Contracting State and satisfy any other conditions specified in the Convention without regard to whether the income is treated as the income of such beneficiaries, members or participants under the tax laws of the first-mentioned Contracting State or such state.

(d) An item of income:

    (i) derived from a Contracting State through an entity that is organized in a state other than the Contracting States; and

    (ii) treated as the income of that entity under the tax laws of the other Contracting State;

shall not be eligible for the benefits of the Convention.

(e) An item of income:

    (i) derived from a Contracting State through an entity that is organized in that Contracting State; and

    (ii) treated as the income of that entity under the tax laws of the other Contracting State;

shall not be eligible for the benefits of the Convention.

ARTICLE 5

1. For the purposes of this Convention, the term "permanent establishment" means a fixed place of business through which the business of an enterprise is wholly or partly carried on.

2. The term "permanent establishment" includes especially:

(a) a place of management;

(b) a branch;

(c) an office;

(d) a factory;

(e) a workshop; and

(f) a mine, an oil or gas well, a quarry or any other place of extraction of natural resources.

3. A building site, a construction or installation project, or an installation or drilling rig or ship used for the exploration of natural resources, constitutes a permanent establishment only if it lasts or the activity continues for a period of more than twelve months.

4. Notwithstanding the preceding provisions of this Article, the term "permanent establishment" shall be deemed not to include:

    (a)   the use of facilities solely for the purpose of storage, display or delivery of goods or merchandise belonging to the enterprise;

    (b)   the maintenance of a stock of goods or merchandise belonging to the enterprise solely for the purpose of storage, display or delivery;

    (c)   the maintenance of a stock of goods or merchandise belonging to the enterprise solely for the purpose of processing by another enterprise;

    (d)   the maintenance of a fixed place of business solely for the purpose of purchasing goods or merchandise or of collecting information, for the enterprise;

    (e)   the maintenance of a fixed place of business solely for the purpose of carrying on, for the enterprise, any other activity of a preparatory or auxiliary character;

    (f)   the maintenance of a fixed place of business solely for any combination of activities mentioned in subparagraphs (a) to (e), provided that the overall activity of the fixed place of business resulting from this combination is of a preparatory or auxiliary character.

5. Notwithstanding the provisions of paragraphs 1 and 2, where a person – other than an agent of an independent status to whom the provisions of paragraph 6 apply – is acting on behalf of an enterprise and has, and habitually exercises, in a Contracting State an authority to conclude contracts in the name of the enterprise, that enterprise shall be deemed to have a permanent establishment in that Contracting State in respect of any activities that the person undertakes for the enterprise, unless the activities of such person are limited to those mentioned in paragraph 4 that, if exercised through a fixed place of business, would not make this fixed place of business a permanent establishment under the provisions of that paragraph.

6. An enterprise shall not be deemed to have a permanent establishment in a Contracting State merely because it carries on business in that Contracting State through a broker, general

commission agent or any other agent of an independent status, provided that such persons are acting in the ordinary course of their business.

7.   The fact that a company which is a resident of a Contracting State controls or is controlled by a company which is a resident of the other Contracting State, or which carries on business in that other Contracting State (whether through a permanent establishment or otherwise), shall not constitute either company a permanent establishment of the other.

ARTICLE 6

1.   Income derived by a resident of a Contracting State from real property (including income from agriculture or forestry) situated in the other Contracting State may be taxed in that other Contracting State.

2.   The term "real property" as used in this Convention shall have the meaning which it has under the laws of the Contracting State in which the property in question is situated. The term shall in any case include property accessory to real property, livestock and equipment used in agriculture and forestry, rights to which the provisions of general law respecting real property apply, usufruct of real property and rights to variable or fixed payments as consideration for the working of, or the right to work, mineral deposits and other natural resources; ships and aircraft shall not be regarded as real property.

3.   The provisions of paragraph 1 shall apply to income derived from the direct use, letting, or use in any other form of real property.

4.   The provisions of paragraphs 1 and 3 shall also apply to the income from real property of an enterprise.

ARTICLE 7

1.   The profits of an enterprise of a Contracting State shall be taxable only in that Contracting State unless the enterprise carries on business in the other Contracting State through a permanent establishment situated therein. If the enterprise carries on business as

aforesaid, the profits of the enterprise may be taxed in that other Contracting State but only so much of them as is attributable to the permanent establishment.

2.   Subject to the provisions of paragraph 3, where an enterprise of a Contracting State carries on business in the other Contracting State through a permanent establishment situated therein, there shall in each Contracting State be attributed to that permanent establishment the profits which it might be expected to make if it were a distinct and separate enterprise engaged in the same or similar activities under the same or similar conditions and dealing wholly independently with the enterprise of which it is a permanent establishment.

3.   In determining the profits of a permanent establishment, there shall be allowed as deductions expenses which are incurred for the purposes of the permanent establishment, including executive and general administrative expenses so incurred, whether in the Contracting State in which the permanent establishment is situated or elsewhere.

4.   Nothing in this Article shall affect the application of any law of a Contracting State relating to the determination of the tax liability of a person in cases where the information available to the competent authority of that Contracting State is inadequate to determine the profits to be attributed to a permanent establishment, provided that, on the basis of the available information, the determination of the profits of the permanent establishment is consistent with the principles stated in this Article.

5.   No profits shall be attributed to a permanent establishment by reason of the mere purchase by that permanent establishment of goods or merchandise for the enterprise.

6.   For the purposes of the preceding paragraphs of this Article, the profits to be attributed to the permanent establishment shall be determined by the same method year by year unless there is good and sufficient reason to the contrary.

7.   Where profits include items of income which are dealt with separately in other Articles of this Convention, then the provisions of those Articles shall not be affected by the provisions of this Article.

ARTICLE 8

1.   Profits from the operation of ships or aircraft in international traffic carried on by an enterprise of a Contracting State shall be taxable only in that Contracting State.

2.   For the purposes of this Article, profits from the operation of ships or aircraft include profits derived from the rental of ships or aircraft on a full basis. They also include profits from the rental of ships or aircraft on a bareboat basis if such rental activities are incidental to the operation of ships or aircraft in international traffic. Profits from the inland transport of property or passengers within either Contracting State shall be treated as profits from the operation of ships or aircraft in international traffic if such transport is undertaken as part of international traffic.

3.   Notwithstanding the provisions of Article 2 and subparagraph (d) of paragraph 1 of Article 3, provided that no political subdivision or local authority of the United States levies a tax similar to the local inhabitant taxes or the enterprise tax in Japan in respect of the operation of ships or aircraft in international traffic carried on by an enterprise of Japan, an enterprise of the United States shall be exempt from the local inhabitant taxes and the enterprise tax in Japan in respect of the operation of ships or aircraft in international traffic.

4.   Profits of an enterprise of a Contracting State from the use, maintenance or rental of containers, including trailers, barges and related equipment for the transport of containers, shall be taxable only in that Contracting State except where such containers are used solely within the other Contracting State.

5.   The provisions of the preceding paragraphs of this Article shall also apply to profits from the participation in a pool, a joint business or an international operating agency.

ARTICLE 9

1.   Where

    (a)   an enterprise of a Contracting State participates directly or indirectly in the management, control or capital of an enterprise of the other Contracting State, or

(b)   the same persons participate directly or indirectly in the management, control or capital of an enterprise of a Contracting State and an enterprise of the other Contracting State,

and in either case conditions are made or imposed between the two enterprises in their commercial or financial relations which differ from those which would be made between independent enterprises, then any profits which would, but for those conditions, have accrued to one of the enterprises, but, by reason of those conditions, have not so accrued, may be included in the profits of that enterprise and taxed accordingly.

2.   Where a Contracting State includes in the profits of an enterprise of that Contracting State – and taxes accordingly – profits on which an enterprise of the other Contracting State has been charged to tax in that other Contracting State and that other Contracting State agrees that the profits so included are profits which would have accrued to the enterprise of the first-mentioned Contracting State if the conditions made between the two enterprises had been those which would have been made between independent enterprises, then that other Contracting State shall make an appropriate adjustment to the amount of the tax charged therein on those profits. In determining such adjustment, due regard shall be had to the other provisions of this Convention.

3.   Notwithstanding the provisions of paragraph 1, a Contracting State shall not change the profits of an enterprise of that Contracting State in the circumstances referred to in that paragraph, if an examination of that enterprise is not initiated within seven years from the end of the taxable year in which the profits that would be subject to such change would, but for the conditions referred to in that paragraph, have accrued to that enterprise. The provisions of this paragraph shall not apply in the case of fraud or willful default or if the inability to initiate an examination within the prescribed period is attributable to the actions or inaction of that enterprise.

ARTICLE 10

1.   Dividends paid by a company which is a resident of a Contracting State to a resident of the other Contracting State may be taxed in that other Contracting State.

2.   However, such dividends may also be taxed in the Contracting State of which the company paying the dividends is a resident and according to the laws of that Contracting State, but if the dividends are beneficially owned by a resident of the other Contracting State, except as provided in paragraphs 4 and 5, the tax so charged shall not exceed:

(a)   5 percent of the gross amount of the dividends if the beneficial owner is a company that owns directly or indirectly, on the date on which entitlement to the dividends is determined, at least 10 percent of the voting stock of the company paying the dividends;

(b)   10 percent of the gross amount of the dividends in all other cases.

This paragraph shall not affect the taxation of the company in respect of the profits out of which the dividends are paid.

3.   Notwithstanding the provisions of paragraph 2, such dividends shall not be taxed in the Contracting State of which the company paying the dividends is a resident if the beneficial owner of the dividends is:

(a)   a company that is a resident of the other Contracting State, that has owned, directly or indirectly through one or more residents of either Contracting State, more than 50 percent of the voting stock of the company paying the dividends for the period of twelve months ending on the date on which entitlement to the dividends is determined, and that either:

(i)   satisfies the conditions described in clause (i) or (ii) of subparagraph (c) of paragraph 1 of Article 22;

(ii)   satisfies the conditions described in clauses (i) and (ii) of subparagraph (f) of paragraph 1 of Article 22, provided that the company satisfies the conditions described in paragraph 2 of that Article with respect to the dividends; or

(iii)   has received a determination pursuant to paragraph 4 of Article 22 with respect to this paragraph; or

(b)   a pension fund that is a resident of the other Contracting State, provided that such dividends are not derived from the carrying on of a business, directly or indirectly, by such pension fund.

4.   The provisions of subparagraph (a) of paragraph 2 and subparagraph (a) of paragraph 3 shall not apply in the case of dividends paid by a United States Regulated Investment Company (hereinafter referred to as a "RIC") or a United States Real Estate Investment Trust (hereinafter referred to as a "REIT"). The provisions of subparagraph (b) of paragraph 2 and subparagraph (b) of paragraph 3 shall apply in the case of dividends paid by a RIC. In the case of dividends paid by a REIT, the provisions of subparagraph (b) of paragraph 2 and subparagraph (b) of paragraph 3 shall apply only if:

(a)   the beneficial owner of the dividends is an individual holding an interest of not more than 10 percent in the REIT or a pension fund holding an interest of not more than 10 percent in the REIT;

(b)   the dividends are paid with respect to a class of stock that is publicly traded and the beneficial owner of the dividends is a person holding an interest of not more than 5 percent of any class of the stock of the REIT; or

(c)   the beneficial owner of the dividends is a person holding an interest of not more than 10 percent in the REIT and that REIT is diversified.

5.   The provisions of subparagraph (a) of paragraph 2 and subparagraph (a) of paragraph 3 shall not apply in the case of dividends paid by a company which is entitled to a deduction for dividends paid to its beneficiaries in computing its taxable income in Japan. The provisions of subparagraph (b) of paragraph 2 and subparagraph (b) of paragraph 3 shall apply in the case of dividends paid by such company, provided that not more than 50 percent of its assets consist, directly or indirectly, of real property situated in Japan. Where more than 50 percent of the assets of such company consist, directly or indirectly, of real property situated in Japan, the provisions of subparagraph (b) of paragraph 2 and subparagraph (b) of paragraph 3 shall apply only if:

(a)   the beneficial owner of the dividends is an individual holding an interest of not more than 10 percent in such company or a pension fund holding an interest of not more than 10 percent in such company;

(b)   the dividends are paid with respect to a class of interest in such company that is publicly traded and the beneficial owner of the dividends is a person holding an interest of not more than 5 percent of any class of interest in the company; or

(c)   the beneficial owner of the dividends is a person holding an interest of not more than 10 percent in the company and the company is diversified.

6.   The term "dividends" as used in this Article means income from shares or other rights, not being debt-claims, participating in profits, as well as income which is subjected to the same taxation treatment as income from shares by the tax laws of the Contracting State of which the payor is a resident.

7.   The provisions of paragraphs 1, 2 and 3 shall not apply if the beneficial owner of the dividends, being a resident of a Contracting State, carries on business in the other Contracting State of which the company paying the dividends is a resident, through a permanent establishment situated therein, and the holding in respect of which the dividends are paid is effectively connected with such permanent establishment. In such case the provisions of Article 7 shall apply.

8.   A Contracting State shall not impose any tax on the dividends paid by a company that is a resident of the other Contracting State, except insofar as the dividends are paid to a resident of the first-mentioned Contracting State or insofar as the holding in respect of which the dividends are paid is effectively connected with a permanent establishment situated in that Contracting State, nor shall it impose tax on a company's undistributed profits, except as provided in paragraph 9, even if the dividends paid or the undistributed profits consist wholly or partly of profits or income arising in that Contracting State.

9.   A company that is a resident of a Contracting State and that has a permanent establishment in the other Contracting State or that is subject to tax in that other Contracting State on its income that may be taxed in that other Contracting State under Article 6 or under paragraph 1 or 2 of Article 13 may be subject in that other Contracting State to a tax in addition

to any tax that may be imposed in that other Contracting State in accordance with the other provisions of this Convention. Such tax, however, may be imposed on only the portion of the profits of the company attributable to the permanent establishment and the portion of the income referred to in the preceding provisions of this paragraph that is subject to tax under Article 6 or under paragraph 1 or 2 of Article 13 that represents the amount of such income that is equivalent to the amount of dividends that would have been paid if such activities had been conducted in a separate legal entity. The provisions of this paragraph shall not apply in the case of a company which:

  (a) satisfies the conditions described in clause (i) or (ii) of subparagraph (c) of paragraph 1 of Article 22;

  (b) satisfies the conditions described in clauses (i) and (ii) of subparagraph (f) of paragraph 1 of Article 22, provided that the company satisfies the conditions described in paragraph 2 of that Article with respect to the income; or

  (c) has received a determination pursuant to paragraph 4 of Article 22 with respect to this paragraph.

10. The tax referred to in paragraph 9 shall not be imposed at a rate in excess of the rate specified in subparagraph (a) of paragraph 2.

11. A resident of a Contracting State shall not be considered the beneficial owner of dividends in respect of preferred stock or other similar interest if such preferred stock or other similar interest would not have been established or acquired unless a person:

  (a) that is not entitled to benefits with respect to dividends paid by a resident of the other Contracting State which are equivalent to, or more favorable than, those available under this Convention to a resident of the first-mentioned Contracting State; and

  (b) that is not a resident of either Contracting State;

held equivalent preferred stock or other similar interest in the first-mentioned resident.

ARTICLE 11

1.   Interest arising in a Contracting State and paid to a resident of the other Contracting State may be taxed in that other Contracting State.

2.   However, such interest may also be taxed in the Contracting State in which it arises and according to the laws of that Contracting State, but if the beneficial owner of the interest is a resident of the other Contracting State, the tax so charged shall not exceed 10 percent of the gross amount of the interest.

3.   Notwithstanding the provisions of paragraph 2, interest arising in a Contracting State shall be taxable only in the other Contracting State if:

(a)   the interest is beneficially owned by that other Contracting State, a political subdivision or local authority thereof, or the central bank of that other Contracting State or any institution wholly owned by that other Contracting State;

(b)   the interest is beneficially owned by a resident of that other Contracting State with respect to debt-claims guaranteed, insured or indirectly financed by the Government of that other Contracting State, a political subdivision or local authority thereof, or the central bank of that other Contracting State or any institution wholly owned by that other Contracting State;

(c)   the interest is beneficially owned by a resident of that other Contracting State that is either:

(i)   a bank (including an investment bank);

(ii)   an insurance company;

(iii)   a registered securities dealer; or

(iv)   any other enterprise, provided that in the three taxable years preceding the taxable year in which the interest is paid, the enterprise derives more than 50 percent of its liabilities from the issuance of bonds in the financial markets or from taking deposits at interest, and more than 50 percent of the assets of the enterprise consist of debt-claims against persons that do not have with the resident a relationship described in subparagraph (a) or (b) of paragraph 1 of Article 9;

(d)   the interest is beneficially owned by a pension fund that is a resident of that other Contracting State, provided that such interest is not derived from the carrying on of a business, directly or indirectly, by such pension fund; or

(e)   the interest is beneficially owned by a resident of that other Contracting State and paid with respect to indebtedness arising as a part of the sale on credit by a resident of that other Contracting State of equipment or merchandise.

4.   For the purposes of paragraph 3, the terms "the central bank" and "institution wholly owned by a Contracting State" mean:

     (a)   in the case of Japan:

          (i)   the Bank of Japan;

          (ii)   the Japan Bank for International Cooperation;

          (iii)   the Nippon Export and Investment Insurance; and

          (iv)   such other similar institution the capital of which is wholly owned by Japan as may be agreed upon from time to time between the Governments of the Contracting States through an exchange of diplomatic notes.

     (b)   in the case of the United States:

          (i)   the Federal Reserve Banks;

          (ii)   the U.S. Export-Import Bank;

          (iii)   the Overseas Private Investment Corporation; and

          (iv)   such other similar institution the capital of which is wholly owned by the United States as may be agreed upon from time to time between the Governments of the Contracting States through an exchange of diplomatic notes.

5.   The term "interest" as used in this Article means income from debt-claims of every kind, whether or not secured by mortgage and whether or not carrying a right to participate in the debtor's profits, and in particular, income from government securities and income from bonds or debentures, including premiums and prizes attaching to such securities, bonds or debentures, and all other income that is subjected to the same taxation treatment as income from money lent by the tax laws of the Contracting State in which the income arises. Income dealt with in Article 10 shall not be regarded as interest for the purposes of this Convention.

6.   The provisions of paragraphs 1, 2 and 3 shall not apply if the beneficial owner of the interest, being a resident of a Contracting State, carries on business in the other Contracting State in which the interest arises, through a permanent establishment situated therein and the debt-claim in respect of which the interest is paid is effectively connected with such permanent establishment. In such case the provisions of Article 7 shall apply.

7.   Interest shall be deemed to arise in a Contracting State when the payor is a resident of that Contracting State. Where, however, the person paying the interest, whether such person is a resident of a Contracting State or not, has in a state other than that of which such person is a resident a permanent establishment in connection with which the indebtedness on which the interest is paid was incurred, and such interest is borne by such permanent establishment, then:

(a)   if the permanent establishment is situated in a Contracting State, such interest shall be deemed to arise in that Contracting State, and

(b)   if the permanent establishment is situated in a state other than the Contracting States, such interest shall not be deemed to arise in either Contracting State.

8.   Where, by reason of a special relationship between the payor and the beneficial owner or between both of them and some other person, the amount of the interest, having regard to the debt-claim for which it is paid, exceeds the amount which would have been agreed upon by the payor and the beneficial owner in the absence of such relationship, the provisions of this Article shall apply only to the last-mentioned amount. In such case, the excess part of the payment may be taxed in the Contracting State in which it arises at a rate not to exceed 5 percent of the gross amount of the excess.

9.   Notwithstanding the provisions of paragraphs 2 and 3, a Contracting State may tax, in accordance with its domestic law, interest paid with respect to the ownership interests in an entity used for the securitization of real estate mortgages or other assets, to the extent that the amount of interest paid exceeds the return on comparable debt instruments as specified by the domestic law of that Contracting State.

10.   Where interest expense is deductible in determining the income of a company that is a resident of a Contracting State, being income which:

(a)   is attributable to a permanent establishment of that company situated in the other

Contracting State; or

(b)   may be taxed in the other Contracting State under Article 6 or paragraph 1 or 2

of Article 13;

and that interest expense exceeds the interest paid by that permanent establishment or paid with

respect to the debt secured by real property situated in that other Contracting State, the amount

of that excess shall be deemed to be interest arising in that other Contracting State and

beneficially owned by a resident of the first-mentioned Contracting State. That deemed interest

may be taxed in that other Contracting State at a rate not to exceed the rate provided for in

paragraph 2, unless the company is described in paragraph 3 in which case it shall be exempt

from such taxation in that other Contracting State.

11.   A resident of a Contracting State shall not be considered the beneficial owner of interest

in respect of a debt-claim if such debt-claim would not have been established unless a person:

(a)   that is not entitled to benefits with respect to interest arising in the other

Contracting State which are equivalent to, or more favorable than, those available under

this Convention to a resident of the first-mentioned Contracting State; and

(b)   that is not a resident of either Contracting State;

held an equivalent debt-claim against the first-mentioned resident.

ARTICLE 12

1.   Royalties arising in a Contracting State and beneficially owned by a resident of the

other Contracting State may be taxed only in that other Contracting State.

2.   The term "royalties" as used in this Article means payments of any kind received as a

consideration for the use of, or the right to use, any copyright of literary, artistic or scientific

work including cinematograph films and films or tapes for radio or television broadcasting, any

patent, trade mark, design or model, plan, or secret formula or process, or for information

concerning industrial, commercial or scientific experience.

3. The provisions of paragraph 1 shall not apply if the beneficial owner of the royalties, being a resident of a Contracting State, carries on business in the other Contracting State in which the royalties arise, through a permanent establishment situated therein, and the right or property in respect of which the royalties are paid is effectively connected with such permanent establishment. In such case the provisions of Article 7 shall apply.

4. Where, by reason of a special relationship between the payor and the beneficial owner or between both of them and some other person, the amount of the royalties, having regard to the use, right or information for which they are paid, exceeds the amount which would have been agreed upon by the payor and the beneficial owner in the absence of such relationship, the provisions of this Article shall apply only to the last-mentioned amount. In such case, the excess part of the payment may be taxed in the Contracting State in which it arises at a rate not to exceed 5 percent of the gross amount of the excess.

5. A resident of a Contracting State shall not be considered the beneficial owner of royalties in respect of the use of intangible property if such royalties would not have been paid to the resident unless the resident pays royalties in respect of the same intangible property to a person:

    (a) that is not entitled to benefits with respect to royalties arising in the other Contracting State which are equivalent to, or more favorable than, those available under this Convention to a resident of the first-mentioned Contracting State; and

    (b) that is not a resident of either Contracting State.

ARTICLE 13

1. Gains derived by a resident of a Contracting State from the alienation of real property situated in the other Contracting State may be taxed in that other Contracting State.

2.   (a) Gains derived by a resident of a Contracting State from the alienation of shares or other comparable rights in a company that is a resident of the other Contracting State and that derives at least 50 percent of its value directly or indirectly from real property situated in that other Contracting State may be taxed in that other Contracting State,

unless the relevant class of shares is traded on a recognized stock exchange specified in subparagraph (b) of paragraph 5 of Article 22 and the resident, and persons related thereto, own in the aggregate 5 percent or less of that class of shares.

(b)   Gains derived by a resident of a Contracting State from the alienation of an interest in a partnership, trust or estate may be taxed in the other Contracting State to the extent that its assets consist of real property situated in that other Contracting State.

3.   (a)   Where

(i)   a Contracting State (including, for this purpose in the case of Japan, the Deposit Insurance Corporation of Japan) provides, pursuant to the domestic law concerning failure resolution involving imminent insolvency of financial institutions in that Contracting State, substantial financial assistance to a financial institution that is a resident of that Contracting State, and

(ii)   a resident of the other Contracting State acquires shares in the financial institution from the first-mentioned Contracting State,

the first-mentioned Contracting State may tax gains derived by the resident of the other Contracting State from the alienation of such shares, provided that the alienation is made within five years from the first date on which such financial assistance was provided.

(b)   The provisions of subparagraph (a) shall not apply if the resident of that other Contracting State acquired any shares in the financial institution from the first-mentioned Contracting State before the entry into force of this Convention or pursuant to a binding contract entered into before the entry into force of the Convention.

4.   Notwithstanding the provisions of paragraphs 2 and 3, gains from the alienation of any property, other than real property, forming part of the business property of a permanent establishment which an enterprise of a Contracting State has in the other Contracting State, including such gains from the alienation of such a permanent establishment (alone or with the whole enterprise), may be taxed in that other Contracting State.

5.   Gains derived by a resident of a Contracting State from the alienation of ships or aircraft operated by that resident in international traffic and any property, other than real

property, pertaining to the operation of such ships or aircraft shall be taxable only in that Contracting State.

6. Gains derived by a resident of a Contracting State from the alienation of containers, including trailers, barges and related equipment for the transport of containers, shall be taxable only in that Contracting State except where such containers were used solely within the other Contracting State.

7. Gains from the alienation of any property other than that referred to in the preceding paragraphs of this Article shall be taxable only in the Contracting State of which the alienator is a resident.

ARTICLE 14

1. Subject to the provisions of Articles 15, 17 and 18, salaries, wages and other similar remuneration derived by a resident of a Contracting State in respect of an employment shall be taxable only in that Contracting State unless the employment is exercised in the other Contracting State. If the employment is so exercised, such remuneration as is derived therefrom may be taxed in that other Contracting State.

2. Notwithstanding the provisions of paragraph 1, remuneration derived by a resident of a Contracting State in respect of an employment exercised in the other Contracting State shall be taxable only in the first-mentioned Contracting State if:

(a) the recipient is present in that other Contracting State for a period or periods not exceeding in the aggregate 183 days in any twelve month period commencing or ending in the taxable year concerned;

(b) the remuneration is paid by, or on behalf of, an employer who is not a resident of that other Contracting State; and

(c) the remuneration is not borne by a permanent establishment which the employer has in that other Contracting State.

3. Notwithstanding the provisions of the preceding paragraphs of this Article, remuneration derived in respect of an employment exercised aboard a ship or aircraft operated

in international traffic by an enterprise of a Contracting State may be taxed in that Contracting State.

ARTICLE 15

Directors' fees and other similar payments derived by a resident of a Contracting State in his capacity as a member of the board of directors of a company which is a resident of the other Contracting State may be taxed in that other Contracting State.

ARTICLE 16

1.   Income derived by an individual who is a resident of a Contracting State as an entertainer, such as a theater, motion picture, radio or television artiste, or a musician, or as a sportsman, from his personal activities as such exercised in the other Contracting State, which income would be exempt from tax in that other Contracting State under the provisions of Articles 7 and 14, may be taxed in that other Contracting State, except where the amount of the gross receipts derived by such entertainer or sportsman, including expenses reimbursed to him or borne on his behalf, from such activities does not exceed ten thousand United States dollars ($10,000) or its equivalent in Japanese yen for the taxable year concerned.

2.   Where income in respect of personal activities exercised in a Contracting State by an individual in his capacity as an entertainer or a sportsman accrues not to the individual himself but to another person that is a resident of the other Contracting State, that income may, notwithstanding the provisions of Articles 7 and 14, be taxed in the Contracting State in which the activities of the individual are exercised, unless the contract pursuant to which the personal activities are performed allows that other person to designate the individual who is to perform the personal activities.

ARTICLE 17

1.   Subject to the provisions of paragraph 2 of Article 18, pensions and other similar remuneration, including social security payments, beneficially owned by a resident of a Contracting State shall be taxable only in that Contracting State.

2.   Annuities derived and beneficially owned by an individual who is a resident of a Contracting State shall be taxable only in that Contracting State. The term "annuities" as used in this paragraph means a stated sum paid periodically at stated times during the life of the individual, or during a specified or ascertainable period of time, under an obligation to make the payments in return for adequate and full consideration (other than services rendered).

3.   Periodic payments, made pursuant to a written separation agreement or a decree of divorce, separate maintenance, or compulsory support, including payments for the support of a child, paid by a resident of a Contracting State to a resident of the other Contracting State shall be taxable only in the first-mentioned Contracting State. However, such payments shall not be taxable in either Contracting State if the individual making such payments is not entitled to a deduction for such payments in computing taxable income in the first-mentioned Contracting State.

ARTICLE 18

1.   (a)   Salaries, wages and other similar remuneration, other than a pension and other similar remuneration, paid by a Contracting State or a political subdivision or local authority thereof to an individual in respect of services rendered to that Contracting State or political subdivision or local authority thereof, in the discharge of functions of a governmental nature, shall be taxable only in that Contracting State.

(b)   However, such salaries, wages and other similar remuneration shall be taxable only in the other Contracting State if the services are rendered in that other Contracting State and the individual is a resident of that other Contracting State who:

(i)   is a national of that other Contracting State; or

(ii)   did not become a resident of that other Contracting State solely for the purpose of rendering the services.

2.   (a)   Any pension and other similar remuneration paid by, or out of funds to which contributions are made by, a Contracting State or a political subdivision or local authority thereof to an individual in respect of services rendered to that Contracting State or a political subdivision or local authority thereof, other than payments made by the United States under provisions of the social security or similar legislation, shall be taxable only in that Contracting State.

(b)   However, such pension and other similar remuneration shall be taxable only in the other Contracting State if the individual is a resident of, and a national of, that other Contacting State.

3.   The provisions of Articles 14, 15, 16 and 17 shall apply to salaries, wages and other similar remuneration, and to pensions and other similar remuneration, in respect of services rendered in connection with a business carried on by a Contracting State or a political subdivision or local authority thereof.

ARTICLE 19

Payments which a student or business apprentice who is, or was immediately before visiting a Contracting State, a resident of the other Contracting State and who is present in the first-mentioned Contracting State for the primary purpose of his education or training receives for the purpose of his maintenance, education or training shall be exempt from tax in the first-mentioned Contracting State, provided that such payments are made to him from outside that first-mentioned Contracting State. The exemption from tax provided by this Article shall apply to a business apprentice only for a period not exceeding one year from the date he first begins his training in the first-mentioned Contracting State.

ARTICLE 20

1.   An individual who visits a Contracting State temporarily for the purpose of teaching or conducting research at a university, college, school or other educational institution in that Contracting State, and who continues to be a resident, within the meaning of paragraph 1 of Article 4, of the other Contracting State, shall be exempt from tax in the first-mentioned Contracting State on any remuneration for such teaching or research for a period not exceeding two years from the date of his arrival.

2.   The provisions of paragraph 1 shall not apply to income from research if such research is undertaken primarily for the private benefit of one or more specific persons.

ARTICLE 21

1.   Items of income beneficially owned by a resident of a Contracting State, wherever arising, not dealt with in the foregoing Articles of this Convention (hereinafter referred to as "other income") shall be taxable only in that Contracting State.

2.   The provisions of paragraph 1 shall not apply to income, other than income from real property, if the beneficial owner of such income, being a resident of a Contracting State, carries on business in the other Contracting State through a permanent establishment situated therein and the right or property in respect of which the income is paid is effectively connected with such permanent establishment. In such case the provisions of Article 7 shall apply.

3.   Where, by reason of a special relationship between the resident referred to in paragraph 1 and the payor, or between both of them and some other person, the amount of other income, having regard to the right or property in respect of which it is paid, exceeds the amount which would have been agreed upon between them in the absence of such relationship, the provisions of this Article shall apply only to the last-mentioned amount. In such case, the excess part of the payment may be taxed in the Contracting State in which it arises at a rate not to exceed 5 percent of the gross amount of the excess.

4.   A resident of a Contracting State shall not be considered the beneficial owner of other income in respect of the right or property if such other income would not have been paid to the

resident unless the resident pays other income in respect of the same right or property to a person:

(a)   that is not entitled to benefits with respect to other income arising in the other Contracting State which are equivalent to, or more favorable than, those available under this Convention to a resident of the first-mentioned Contracting State; and

(b)   that is not a resident of either Contracting State.

ARTICLE 22

1.   Except as otherwise provided in this Article, a resident of a Contracting State that derives income from the other Contracting State shall be entitled to all the benefits accorded to residents of a Contracting State for a taxable year by the provisions of other Articles of this Convention only if such resident satisfies any other specified conditions for the obtaining of such benefits and is either:

(a)   an individual;

(b)   a Contracting State, any political subdivision or local authority thereof, the Bank of Japan or the Federal Reserve Banks;

(c)   a company, if:

     (i)   the principal class of its shares, and any disproportionate class of its shares, is listed or registered on a recognized stock exchange specified in clause (i) or (ii) of subparagraph (b) of paragraph 5 and is regularly traded on one or more recognized stock exchanges; or

     (ii)   at least 50 percent of each class of shares in the company is owned directly or indirectly by five or fewer residents entitled to benefits under clause (i), provided that, in the case of indirect ownership, each intermediate owner is a person entitled to the benefits of this Convention under this paragraph;

(d)   a person described in subparagraph (c) of paragraph 1 of Article 4;

(e)   a pension fund, provided that as of the end of the prior taxable year more than

50 percent of its beneficiaries, members or participants are individuals who are

residents of either Contracting State; or

(f)   a person other than an individual, if:

    (i)   residents that are described in subparagraph (a), (b), (d) or (e), or clause

    (i) of subparagraph (c), own, directly or indirectly, at least 50 percent of each

    class of shares or other beneficial interests in the person, and

    (ii)   less than 50 percent of the person's gross income for the taxable year is

    paid or accrued by the person in that taxable year, directly or indirectly, to

    persons who are not residents of either Contracting State in the form of

    payments that are deductible in computing its taxable income in the Contracting

    State of which it is a resident (but not including arm's length payments in the

    ordinary course of business for services or tangible property and payments in

    respect of financial obligations to a commercial bank, provided that where such

    a bank is not a resident of a Contracting State such payment is attributable to a

    permanent establishment of that bank situated in one of the Contracting States).

2.   (a)   A resident of a Contracting State shall be entitled to benefits of this Convention

with respect to an item of income derived from the other Contracting State if the

resident is engaged in the first-mentioned Contracting State in the active conduct of a

trade or business, other than the business of making or managing investments for the

resident's own account, unless these activities are banking, insurance or securities

activities carried on by a commercial bank, insurance company or registered securities

dealer, the income derived from the other Contracting State is derived in connection

with, or is incidental to, that trade or business and that resident satisfies any other

specified conditions for the obtaining of such benefits.

(b)   If a resident of a Contracting State derives an item of income from a trade or

business activity in the other Contracting State, or derives an item of income arising in

the other Contracting State from a person that has with the resident a relationship

described in subparagraph (a) or (b) of paragraph 1 of Article 9, the conditions described in subparagraph (a) shall be considered to be satisfied with respect to such item only if the trade or business activity carried on by the resident in the first-mentioned Contracting State is substantial in relation to the trade or business activity carried on by the resident or such person in the other Contracting State. Whether a trade or business activity is substantial for the purposes of this paragraph will be determined based on all the facts and circumstances.

3.   (a)   Where the provisions of clause (ii) of subparagraph (c) of paragraph 1 apply in respect of taxation by withholding at source, a resident of a Contracting State shall be considered to satisfy the conditions described in that clause for a taxable year in which the payment is made if such resident satisfies those conditions during the part of that taxable year which precedes the date of payment of the item of income (or, in the case of dividends, the date on which entitlement to the dividends is determined) and, unless that date is the last day of that taxable year, during the whole of the preceding taxable year.

   (b)   Where the provisions of clause (i) of subparagraph (f) of paragraph 1 apply:

      (i)   in respect of taxation by withholding at source, a resident of a Contracting State shall be considered to satisfy the conditions described in that clause for a taxable year in which the payment is made if such resident satisfies those conditions during the part of that taxable year which precedes the date of payment of the item of income (or, in the case of dividends, the date on which entitlement to the dividends is determined) and, unless that date is the last day of that taxable year, during the whole of the preceding taxable year; and

      (ii)   in all other cases, a resident of a Contracting State shall be considered to satisfy the conditions described in that clause for a taxable year in which the payment is made if such resident satisfies those conditions on at least half the days of the taxable year.

   (c)   Where the provisions of clause (ii) of subparagraph (f) of paragraph 1 apply in respect of taxation by withholding at source in Japan, a resident of the United States shall be considered to satisfy the conditions described in that subparagraph for a taxable year in which the payment is made if such resident satisfies those conditions for the three taxable years preceding that taxable year.

4.   A resident of a Contracting State that is not described in paragraph 1 and is not entitled to benefits with respect to an item of income under paragraph 2 shall, nevertheless, be granted benefits of this Convention if the competent authority of the Contracting State from which benefits are claimed determines, in accordance with its domestic law or administrative practice, that the establishment, acquisition or maintenance of such resident and the conduct of its operations are considered as not having the obtaining of benefits under the Convention as one of its principal purposes.

5.   For the purposes of this Article:

(a)   the term "disproportionate class of shares" means any class of shares of a company that is a resident of a Contracting State which is subject to terms or other arrangements that entitle the holders of that class of shares to a portion of the income of the company derived from the other Contracting State that is larger than the portion such holders would receive absent such terms or arrangements;

(b)   the term "recognized stock exchange" means:

(i)   any stock exchange established under the terms of the Securities and Exchange Law (Law No. 25 of 1948) of Japan;

(ii)   the NASDAQ System and any stock exchange registered with the Securities and Exchange Commission as a national securities exchange under the Securities Exchange Act of 1934 of the United States; and

(iii)   any other stock exchange agreed upon by the competent authorities; and

(c)   the term "gross income" means the total revenues derived by a resident of a Contracting State from its business, less the direct costs of obtaining such revenues.

ARTICLE 23

1.   Subject to the provisions of the laws of Japan regarding the allowance as a credit against the Japanese tax of tax payable in any country other than Japan:

(a)   Where a resident of Japan derives income from the United States which may be taxed in the United States in accordance with the provisions of this Convention, the amount of the United States tax payable in respect of that income shall be allowed as a credit against the Japanese tax imposed on that resident. The amount of credit, however, shall not exceed that part of the Japanese tax which is appropriate to that income.

(b)   Where the income derived from the United States is dividends paid by a company which is a resident of the United States to a company which is a resident of Japan and which owns not less than 10 percent of the voting shares issued by the company paying the dividends during the period of six months immediately before the day when the obligation to pay dividends is confirmed, the credit shall take into account the United States tax payable by the company paying the dividends in respect of its income.

For the purposes of this paragraph, income beneficially owned by a resident of Japan which may be taxed in the United States in accordance with the Convention shall be deemed to arise from sources in the United States.

2.   In accordance with the provisions and subject to the limitations of the laws of the United States (as it may be amended from time to time without changing the general principle hereof), the United States shall allow to a resident or citizen of the United States as a credit against the United States tax on income:

(a)   the Japanese tax paid or accrued by or on behalf of such citizen or resident; and

(b)   in the case of a company that is a resident of the United States and that owns at least 10 percent of the voting stock of a company that is a resident of Japan and from which the first-mentioned company receives dividends, the Japanese tax paid or accrued by or on behalf of the payor with respect to the profits out of which the dividends are paid.

For the purposes of this paragraph, the taxes referred to in subparagraph (a) of paragraph 1 and paragraph 2 of Article 2 shall be considered Japanese taxes imposed on the beneficial owner of the income. For the purposes of this paragraph, an item of gross income, as determined under the laws of the United States, derived by a resident of the United States that, under this Convention, may be taxed in Japan shall be deemed to be income from sources in Japan.

3.   For the purposes of applying the preceding paragraphs of this Article, where the United States taxes, in accordance with paragraph 4 of Article 1, a citizen, or a former citizen or long-term resident, of the United States who is a resident of Japan:

(a)   Japan shall take into account for the purposes of computing the credit to be allowed under paragraph 1 only the amount of tax that the United States may impose on income under the provisions of this Convention that is derived by a resident of Japan who is neither a citizen, nor a former citizen nor long-term resident, of the United States;

(b)   for the purposes of computing the United States tax on income referred to in subparagraph (a), the United States shall allow as a credit against the United States tax the Japanese tax after the credit referred to in that subparagraph; the credit so allowed shall not reduce the portion of the United States tax that is creditable against the Japanese tax in accordance with that subparagraph; and

(c)   for the exclusive purpose of allowing the credit by the United States provided for under subparagraph (b), income referred to in subparagraph (a) shall be deemed to arise in Japan to the extent necessary to allow the United States to grant the credit provided for in subparagraph (b).

ARTICLE 24

1.   Nationals of a Contracting State shall not be subjected in the other Contracting State to any taxation or any requirement connected therewith, which is other or more burdensome than the taxation and connected requirements to which nationals of that other Contracting State in the same circumstances, in particular with respect to taxation on worldwide income, are or may be subjected. The provisions of this paragraph shall also apply to persons who are not residents of one or both of the Contracting States.

2.   The taxation on a permanent establishment which an enterprise of a Contracting State has in the other Contracting State shall not be less favorably levied in that other Contracting State than the taxation levied on enterprises of that other Contracting State carrying on the same activities. The provisions of this paragraph shall not be construed as obliging a Contracting State to grant to residents of the other Contracting State any personal allowances, reliefs and reductions for taxation purposes on account of civil status or family responsibilities which it grants to its own residents.

3.   Except where the provisions of paragraph 1 of Article 9, paragraph 8 of Article 11, paragraph 4 of Article 12, or paragraph 3 of Article 21 apply, interest, royalties and other disbursements paid by a resident of a Contracting State to a resident of the other Contracting State shall, for the purposes of determining the taxable profits of the first-mentioned resident, be deductible under the same conditions as if they had been paid to a resident of the first-mentioned Contracting State. Similarly, any debts of a resident of a Contracting State to a resident of the other Contracting State shall, for the purposes of determining the taxable capital of the first-mentioned resident, be deductible under the same conditions as if they had been contracted to a resident of the first-mentioned Contracting State.

4.   Enterprises of a Contracting State, the capital of which is wholly or partly owned or controlled, directly or indirectly, by one or more residents of the other Contracting State, shall not be subjected in the first-mentioned Contracting State to any taxation or any requirement connected therewith which is other or more burdensome than the taxation and connected requirements to which other similar enterprises of the first-mentioned Contracting State are or may be subjected.

5.   Nothing in this Article shall be construed as preventing either Contracting State from imposing a tax as described in paragraph 9 of Article 10 or paragraph 10 of Article 11.

6.   The provisions of this Article shall, notwithstanding the provisions of Article 2 and subparagraph (d) of paragraph 1 of Article 3, apply to taxes of every kind and description imposed by a Contracting State or a political subdivision or local authority thereof.

ARTICLE 25

1.   Where a person considers that the actions of one or both of the Contracting States result or will result for him in taxation not in accordance with the provisions of this Convention, he may, irrespective of the remedies provided by the domestic law of those Contracting States, present his case to the competent authority of the Contracting State of which he is a resident or, if his case comes under paragraph 1 of Article 24, to that of the Contracting State of which he is a national. The case must be presented within three years from the first notification of the action resulting in taxation not in accordance with the provisions of the Convention.

2.   The competent authority shall endeavor, if the objection appears to it to be justified and if it is not itself able to arrive at a satisfactory solution, to resolve the case by mutual agreement with the competent authority of the other Contracting State, with a view to the avoidance of taxation which is not in accordance with the provisions of this Convention. Any agreement reached shall be implemented notwithstanding any time limits or other procedural limitations in the domestic law of the Contracting States, except such limitations as apply for the purposes of giving effect to such an agreement.

3.   The competent authorities of the Contracting States shall endeavor to resolve by mutual agreement any difficulties or doubts arising as to the interpretation or application of this Convention. In particular the competent authorities of the Contracting States may agree:

    (a)   to the same attribution of income, deductions, credits, or allowances of an
    enterprise of a Contracting State to its permanent establishment situated in the other
    Contracting State;

    (b)   to the same allocation of income, deductions, credits, or allowances between
    persons;

    (c)   to the settlement of conflicting application of the Convention, including
    conflicts regarding:

        (i)   the characterization of particular items of income;

        (ii)   the characterization of persons;

        (iii)   the application of source rules with respect to particular items of income;
        and

(iv)   the meaning of any term used in the Convention; and

(d)   to advance pricing arrangements.

They may also consult together for the elimination of double taxation in cases not provided for in the Convention.

4.   The competent authorities of the Contracting States may communicate with each other directly for the purposes of reaching an agreement in the sense of the preceding paragraphs of this Article.

ARTICLE 26

1.   The competent authorities of the Contracting States shall exchange such information as is relevant for carrying out the provisions of this Convention or of the domestic law of the Contracting States concerning taxes of every kind and description imposed by a Contracting State insofar as the taxation thereunder is not contrary to the provisions of the Convention. The exchange of information is not restricted by paragraph 1 of Article 1. If specifically requested by the competent authority of a Contracting State, the competent authority of the other Contracting State shall provide information under this Article in the form of authenticated copies of original documents (including books, papers, statements, records, accounts, and writings).

2.   Any information received under paragraph 1 by a Contracting State shall be treated as secret in the same manner as information obtained under the domestic law of that Contracting State and shall be disclosed only to persons or authorities (including courts and administrative bodies) involved in the assessment, collection or administration of, the enforcement or prosecution in respect of, or the determination of appeals in relation to, the taxes referred to in the first sentence of paragraph 1, or to supervisory bodies, and only to the extent necessary for those persons, authorities or supervisory bodies to perform their respective responsibilities. Such persons, authorities or supervisory bodies shall use the information only for the purposes of discharging such responsibilities. They may disclose the information in public court proceedings or in judicial decisions.

3.   In no case shall the provisions of the preceding paragraphs of this Article be construed so as to impose on a Contracting State the obligation:

     (a)   to carry out administrative measures at variance with the laws and administrative practice of that or of the other Contracting State;

     (b)   to supply information which is not obtainable under the laws or in the normal course of the administration of that or of the other Contracting State;

     (c)   to supply information which would disclose any trade, business, industrial, commercial or professional secret or trade process, or information, the disclosure of which would be contrary to public policy (ordre public).

4.   In order to effectuate the exchange of information as provided in paragraph 1, each Contracting State shall take necessary measures, including legislation, rule-making, or administrative arrangement, to ensure that its competent authority has sufficient powers under its domestic law to obtain information for the exchange of information regardless of whether that Contracting State may need such information for purposes of its own tax.

5.   The provisions of this Article shall, notwithstanding the provisions of Article 2 and subparagraph (d) of paragraph 1 of Article 3, apply to taxes of every kind and description imposed by a Contracting State insofar as the taxation thereunder is not contrary to the provisions of this Convention.

ARTICLE 27

1.   Each of the Contracting States shall endeavor to collect such taxes imposed by the other Contracting State as will ensure that any exemption or reduced rate of tax granted under this Convention by that other Contracting State shall not be enjoyed by persons not entitled to such benefits. The Contracting State making such collections shall be responsible to the other Contracting State for the sums thus collected.

2.   In no case shall the provisions of paragraph 1 be construed so as to impose upon either of the Contracting States endeavoring to collect the taxes the obligation to carry out administrative measures at variance with the laws and administrative practice of that

Contracting State or which would be contrary to the public policy (ordre public) of that Contracting State.

ARTICLE 28

Nothing in this Convention shall affect the fiscal privileges of members of diplomatic missions or consular posts under the general rules of international law or under the provisions of special agreements.

ARTICLE 29

If a Contracting State considers that a substantial change in the laws relevant to this Convention has been or will be made in the other Contracting State, the first-mentioned Contracting State may make a request to that other Contracting State in writing for consultations with a view to determining the possible effect of such change on the balance of benefits provided by the Convention and, if appropriate, to amending the provisions of the Convention to arrive at an appropriate balance of benefits. The requested Contracting State shall enter into consultations with the requesting Contracting State within three months from the date on which the request is received by the requested Contracting State.

ARTICLE 30

1.   This Convention shall be subject to ratification, and the instruments of ratification shall be exchanged as soon as possible. It shall enter into force on the date of the exchange of instruments of ratification.

2.   This Convention shall be applicable:

    (a)   in Japan:

        (i)   with respect to taxes withheld at source:

(aa)   for amounts taxable on or after July 1 of the calendar year in which the Convention enters into force, if the Convention enters into force before April 1 of a calendar year; or

(bb)   for amounts taxable on or after January 1 of the calendar year next following the year in which the Convention enters into force, if the Convention enters into force after March 31 of a calendar year; and

(ii)   with respect to taxes on income which are not withheld at source and the enterprise tax, as regards income for any taxable year beginning on or after January 1 of the calendar year next following that in which the Convention enters into force; and

(b)   in the United States:

(i)   with respect to taxes withheld at source:

(aa)   for amounts paid or credited on or after July 1 of the calendar year in which the Convention enters into force, if the Convention enters into force before April 1 of a calendar year; or

(bb)   for amounts paid or credited on or after January 1 of the calendar year next following the date on which the Convention enters into force, if the Convention enters into force after March 31 of a calendar year; and

(ii)   with respect to other taxes, for taxable periods beginning on or after January 1 of the calendar year next following the date on which the Convention enters into force.

3.   Notwithstanding the entry into force of this Convention, an individual who was entitled to the benefits of Article 19 or 20 of the Convention between the United States of America and Japan for the Avoidance of Double Taxation and the Prevention of Fiscal Evasion with respect to Taxes on Income, signed on March 8, 1971 (hereinafter referred to as "the prior Convention") at the time of the entry into force of this Convention shall continue to be entitled to such benefits until such time as the individual would cease to be entitled to such benefits if the prior Convention remained in force.

4.   The prior Convention shall cease to have effect in relation to any tax from the date on which this Convention has effect in relation to that tax in accordance with paragraphs 1 and 2. Notwithstanding the preceding provisions of this paragraph, where any person entitled to benefits under the prior Convention would have been entitled to greater benefits thereunder than under this Convention, the prior Convention shall, at the election of such person, continue to have effect in its entirety for the period of twelve months from the date on which the provisions of this Convention otherwise would have effect under paragraph 2. The prior Convention shall terminate on the last date on which it has effect in relation to any tax in accordance with the preceding provisions of this paragraph.

ARTICLE 31

This Convention shall remain in force until terminated by a Contracting State. Either Contracting State may terminate the Convention after the expiration of a period of five years from the date of its entry into force, by giving to the other Contracting State, through the diplomatic channel, six months prior written notice of termination. In such event, the Convention shall cease to have effect:

(a)   in Japan:

(i)   with respect to taxes withheld at source, for amounts taxable on or after January 1 of the calendar year next following the expiration of the six month period; and

(ii)   with respect to taxes on income which are not withheld at source and the enterprise tax, as regards income for any taxable year beginning on or after January 1 of the calendar year next following the expiration of the six month period; and

(b)   in the United States:

(i)   with respect to taxes withheld at source, for amounts paid or credited on or after January 1 of the calendar year next following the expiration of the six month period; and

(ii)   with respect to other taxes, for taxable periods beginning on or after

January 1 of the calendar year next following the expiration of the six month

period.

IN WITNESS WHEREOF the undersigned, being duly authorized thereto by their

respective Governments, have signed this Convention.

DONE in duplicate at Washington this sixth day of November, 2003, in the English and

Japanese languages, each text being equally authentic.

FOR THE GOVERNMENT OF   FOR THE GOVERNMENT OF
THE UNITED STATES OF AMERICA: JAPAN:

www.ingramcontent.com/pod-product-compliance
Lightning Source LLC
Chambersburg PA
CBHW071343310526
45790CB00018B/1162